VERNACULAR HISTORY SERIES NO 4

THE DIARY OF JANE GLENN

D1583772

VERNACULAR HISTORY SERIES

The 'Vernacular History' series of books and booklets, of which this is number four, gives a picture of life 'as it really was'—or at least as it seemed to be to those living it at the time: and the time may be as early as the first decade of the twentieth century, or possibly even earlier, up to the quite recent past. There is no precise time of 'cut-off' and the intention of the series is to show life as it was experienced by those involved—and perhaps to correct impressions given by fictional events in a fictional landscape. The series is similar to the **Life in Lincolnshire** series except that the scene is not necessarily restricted to a Lincolnshire setting and titles may vary very considerably in length. The criterion for acceptance into the series is essentially personal experience. Polished literary exposition may or may not be present—veracity is mandatory.

These accounts may sometimes be the work of men and women experienced in writing but also they may sometimes be the work of those who have not had the benefits of extended formal education and have never previously written for publication. So far as practicable editing has been kept to a minimum with the account being presented in the words of the author and any illustration being from contemporary material. Although memories are not infallible, and some recollected detail may have become embroidered with the passage of time, the books are intended as factual records of the experiences of men and women, in all social groups, which might not otherwise have been preserved. There can hardly be any more accurate record of the experiences of life than a personal diary written solely for personal record without any thought of publication. Such is this diary.

No 1. — LIFE ON THE TRENT AND HUMBER RIVERS

No 2. — ALL THIS AND NO MILK
A TALE OF LIFE IN THE HOLBEACH MARSHES – 1933-35

No 3. — BOSTON OUT OF SIGHT

No 4. — THE DIARY OF JANE GLENN

THE DIARY OF JANE GLENN

OF

RUSKINGTON

IN THE

COUNTY OF LINCOLN

FOR THE YEAR 1917

(FROM MONDAY 8TH JANUARY 1917 – SUNDAY 6TH JANUARY 1918)

Transcribed and Introduced

by

Derrick Wood

1970   1996

Richard Kay
80 Sleaford Road • Boston • Lincolnshire • PE21 8EU

First published in 1996
by Richard Kay Publications

ISBN 0 902662 47 3

© Diary: Legatee of estate of Jane Glenn
© Introduction, notes, and transcribed format: Derrick Wood

Reprinted December 2003

Files manipulated via Microsoft Word™ and PageMaker™ on an AppleMacintosh and output in PostScript™ files which were converted to Interpress™ on Rank Xerox Media Server. Printed electronically, in Bookman typeface for the body of the text, at 600 dpi resolution at 135 pages per minute on a Rank Xerox DocuTech™ 135 Laser Production Publishing System by:

Foxe Laser
Enterprise Road • Mablethorpe • Lincolnshire. LN12 1NB

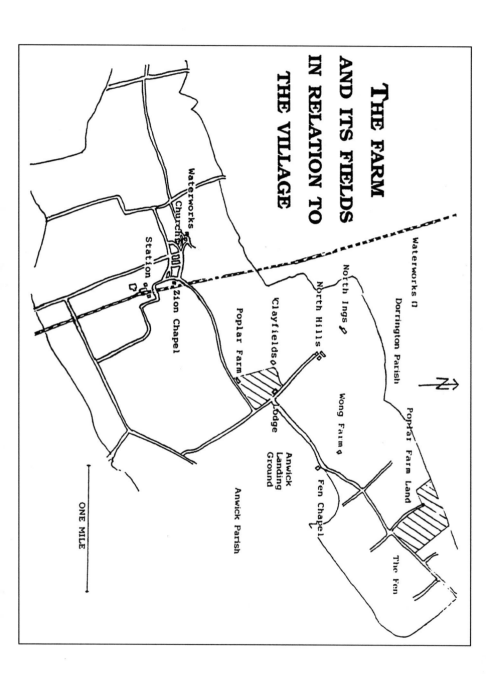

THE FARM
AND ITS FIELDS
IN RELATION TO
THE VILLAGE

Waterworks

Church

Station

Zion Chapel

Waterworks

Dorrington Parish

North Ings

North Hills

Poplar Farm

Clayfields

Lodge

Wong Farm

Anwick
Landing
Ground

Fen Chapel

Poplar Farm Land

The Fen

Anwick Parish

N

ONE MILE

INTRODUCTION

Whilst engaged on a study of local history I was offered the loan of the original diary, and I immediately recognised that it was a unique record of Ruskington village life during the Great War of 1914-1918. Not only does it give a detailed account of the farming of the time, it also describes the rich social life of the members of the Wesleyan Reform Church, and in particular the activities of the close-knit Glenn family and their workers.

The effects of the war upon the village are clearly shown in the daily records and are beautifully summarised at the end of the diary.

I have copied the entries exactly as written, the few mistakes which Jane made are insignificant when we realise that she probably left school at twelve years of age.

It has been a great privilege to read and work on the diary and I am grateful to David Murray, Jane's nephew, both for lending it to me and for his assistance on several points.

I also wish to thank my wife Ruth, and the following friends for their valuable help and advice, Mrs Ida Clarricoates, Miss Una Newton, Mr & Mrs George Phillips, and Mr N. Silson.

Derrick Wood
1996

Notes on the Farms Mentioned in the Diary.

The Ruskington Poor Book of 1896 shows that Robt. Henry Glenn occupied 139 acres in the Clayfield.

In 1916 each occupier of land had to complete a return of his crops and livestock, as the food supply was in danger from the attacks on shipping by enemy submarines. Joseph Glenn had 66 acres in Clayfields, of which 32 acres were grassland, 12 acres were sown with wheat and there were another 22 acres of arable land. He had two horses, four cows in milk, six yarded cattle and four pigs.

Hy. Robert Glenn had Poplar Farm of 118.5 acres, with 51 acres of grassland, 24.5 acres of wheat, and 43 acres of arable land. He had eight horses, two cows in milk and two dry, ten yarded cattle and three others, three sows and four other pigs.

———o———

The Chief Characters in the Diary.

HENRY ROBERT GLENN occupied Poplar Farm and lived to 90 years of age. He and his wife MARY ANN had the following children.

MARY who married Harry Silson: see below.
TOM who farmed at Dorrington.
JANE the diarist.
LIZZIE who married Geo. Harsley.
LILIAN who was appointed a monitress at the Infant School from 1st December 1913. She attended classes at Ruskington Voluntary School twice a week from Jan. 1915 and later went for lessons to a school in Sleaford and also had private tuition. In 1918 she was appointed as a Supplementary Teacher at

Brauncewell School. Later she married Jim Murray, see below.
JOSEPH GLENN the brother of Henry Robert, occupied Clayfields Farm, his children were :-

WILLIAM (Will) who was wounded in The Great War and later had a cobbler's shop in Dorrington.
JOSEPH (Joey) and HENRY who later, together farmed Clayfields.

MARY SILSON née GLENN had the following children :-

ARNOLD who emigrated to New Zealand: now deceased.
GEORGE had the general store in Millview Road, also deceased.
RUTH lives at Irchester.
ROBERT lives at Branston.
IDA whose birth is recorded in the diary, and who married George Clarricoates, lives in the village.
JOYCE lives in Yorkshire.
NORMAN now retired and living in the village.

BRIGADIER MURRAY an officer of the Salvation Army whose son,
JIM MURRAY, came as a pupil to Poplar Farm and married Lilian Glenn. They had one son, David, who now occupies Highfield Farm.

LEWIS ABBOTT came from Newark and lived at North Hills whilst working at Poplar Farm, he married Naomi Phillips who died in 1993 at the age of 99.

HARRIETT PHILLIPS was a dressmaker.

Mr LOBB was the Minister of The Wesleyan Reform Chapel in Ruskington Fen.

Miss ELIZABETH CUNNINGTON was the Headmistress of Ruskington Infants School.
Miss ANNIE CUNNINGTON was her sister.

Jane's parents: Henry Robert and Mary Ann Glenn

In the stackyard at Poplar Farm–posed for the cameraman

DIARY

FOR THE YEAR 1917

COMMENCING ON MONDAY 8TH DAY OF JANUARY

Monday 8 January: Dad cycled to Market came on Snow bitterly cold left His cycle at Hooton's & ride home with Tom. Lilian cycled through it.

Tuesday 9 January: Wash day I helped to feed things.

Wednesday 10 January: Not very well. Had a dreadful headache. Aeroplane came down at Landing stage.[1] Went to see it. 1st I had seen down, saw him start off again. Came from Melton Mowbray.

Thursday 11 January: Very poorly. Mr Lobb came for dinner. Service here—Only Joey came I couldn't sit up for Service. Had to go to bed.

Friday 12 January: Very poorly could not breathe very well all day. Lizzie went Mangold Cleaning at Mr Harphams mangolds.[2] Misses Cunnington came for tea. Lilian left cycle and came home by Train Snowy.

Saturday 13 January: A little better. Got up for tea. Lilian went to Leasingham to see if Mr Smith would take Aft. for me. Killed Pig (Mr Seward) Lizzie went Cleaning Mangolds—Put Truck on 5 Tons 8 Cwts

Sunday 14 January: Snowy no children came all day. Preacher Tom. I was planned Leasingham—Mr Smith took Aft, Harry Night. I was little better got up for dinner. Had Service Home Jim conducted and spoke. Lilian read lesson—it was nice.

---

[1] This was the Anwick Emergency Landing Ground situated off Ruskington Fen Road and now marked by a plaque. 38 Squadron, based at Melton Mowbray, were responsible for the landing ground and flew BE2e and FE2b pusher bi-planes against every known Zeppelin intruding into Midlands airspace but without success.

[2] Mangolds (Mangel-Wurzels)–A root crop; variety of beet grown to feed to animals in winter.

Monday 15 January: Man came to cut Pig up. Dad went to Market rode with Mr Cook, bought me this Diary. Lilian walked to Sleaford cycled home.

Tuesday 16 January: Made Sausages Pork Pies etc. I was able to help a little. Lilian walked to school and trained home.

Wednesday 17 January: Baking Helped with pies.

Thursday 18 January: Not quite so well today. Washed.

Friday 19 January: Better again. Helping in house. Great factory explosion at London.[3] Heard the explosion here quite plainly 7 o'clock. Thought at first it was Zepps.

Saturday 20 January: Helping a little in house. Arnold brought Papers. Harry called went to Kitty's. Very cold and sleety.

Sunday 21 January: Misses Cunnington and Miss Pridmore came aft. Preacher Mr Lawson. I went as far as Lodge[4] and came back. Jim led Service at Home. Lilian Spoke. Preacher went to Pouchers

Monday 22 January: Went and fetched Paper from Mary's. Lizzie fetched Boys Home to fetch Manure from Stn.[5] New Plans and Magazines came

Tuesday 23 January: Boys went Mangold cleaning (Harphams) I took Will's parcel to post. Met Luie coming to see me, walked back with me. Saw an Airship.

Wednesday 24 January: Went for walk twice. Very cold. Was to go to Mary's but did not feel well enough. Dad went to see if he could have truck

Thursday 25th January: Boys went cleaning Mangolds (Harphams) Lizzie had to go cleaning send Lewis Home to go to Stn. with 2 loads because of truck.

---

[3] On 19 January there was a major munitions' factory explosion at the Venesta works in London in which 69 people were killed. It was heard in Salisbury, some 90 miles west of London. Ruskington is about 110 miles north of London. It seems quite possible that it was indeed heard in Ruskington.

[4] On the Fen Road at the entrance to the North Hills farm.

[5] The 'manure' would probably have been an artificial fertiliser such as suplhate of ammonia which was a by-product from gas works.

Friday 26 January: Went to Auntie's for some milk. Very cold. Hay presser[6] came in for cup of tea said He married Mr Proctor's daughter Emma. Put truck mangolds on 5 tons 6 cwts.

Saturday 27 January: Helping in the House. A week of very cold sharp weather.

Sunday 28 January: Went to Chapel twice Preacher Mr Hewerdine. Service at Home Leader Jim, Speaker Lizzie.

Monday 29 January: Dad and Mother went to Market. Mother bought new dress and Blouse Lilian two blouses. Saw airship twice. Boys went sliding on pond in grass field.

Tuesday 30 January: Wash day. Brigadier Murray[7]. came by 6.30 from Lincoln.

Wednesday 31 January: Jim took His Father to meet first train. Mr Lobb came to tea went with Jim to Heckington to help in Entertainment.

Thursday 1 February: Leading fodder to Stn. I made up 1000 words from the One word Demobilisation. Jim promised me 1d Lewis 2d if I did. Shall put it in Missionary Box when I get it.

Friday 2 February: Lizzie went to help Mary. Started Pegging Rug for Bedroom. Wrote to Will, for Auntie, Very anxious not hearing from him, five parcels sent & no word about them.

Saturday 3 February: Lewis and Naomi went to Newark to see His Mother then to Syerston to see Aunt. Another week's frost & Snow. Lizzie and Lilian went to fetch my Boots Paper Etc Georgie's birthday 6th.

Sunday 4 February: Fall of Snow about 3 ins. No Children came. Preacher Mr W. Kelly. Rook Calved. Service at Home.

Monday 5 February: Lilian went to school with Cutlers trained

---

[6] A hay presser was a man who went around the farms baling hay.

[7] Brigadier Murray belonged to the Salvation Army in which he served for many years. He was the father of Jim mentioned above and the grandfather of Mr David Murray.

Home. Lizzie poorly Cleaned few Mangolds very frozen.
Tuesday 6 February: Very sharp Lilian trained to school.
Lizzie much better fetched paper.   We had letter from Will
& letter & P for Home.   Got their first parcel and ours.
Wednesday 7 February: Lizzie went to help Mary with little
Pigs.   Arnold brought Paper.   Jack Poucher came stayed
dinner.   Lilian went to Harriets.   I stayed in all day.   Very
sharp frost, all waters indoors and out frozed.   Rhyme not
gone off trees and hedges all day.   Did little pegging.   38
yrs today since Aunt (Ann) died Dad oldest sister.   Schools
closed cannot get coke.
Thursday 8 February: Lizzie went to help Mary.   Lilian at
Home.   Got nice lot of Pegging done.   Lilian, Arnold and
Henry went sliding on Grass Field Pond.
Friday 9 February: Mr Lobb came to see Dad.   Lizzie came
home from Mary's.   Cleaned some Mangolds & helped to
Chaff[8] cut.   Mary and Children came up.   Lilian trained
to School.   Lewis and Naomi came Home.
Saturday 10 February: Raw and Foggy.   Helping in the House.
Thrashing Machine came[9].   Very Sharp and Frosty all the
Week.   Beck frozen all the week.
Sunday 11 February: Preacher Mr Clay did not come morn,
Dad took Service Very good congregations Service at
Home.   Jim conducted and spoke a Very nice Service.
Monday 12 February: Thrashing Barley (14 qrs. good).   Mrs
Start and Uncle Joe helping us.   A lovely day, finished in
good time first full days work I have done for six weeks.
Jack went back again to Plymouth.
Tuesday 13 February: Wash day.   Thrasher went to
Scotchmans.   Dad went down Fen, Anwick and Sleaford
on his Cycle.   Had a cold.   I helped to feed things & cut

---

[8] The straw, usually barley, was chopped into short lengths and mixed with chopped mangolds for cattle feed. Oat straw was used for the horses.
[9] A contractor hauled the threshing machine from farm to farm by means of a steam engine before combine harvesters were made. The grain was separated from the straw, winnowed, graded for size and delivered into bags.

chaff. Miss Cunningtons called. Lilian stayed Sleaford to go to Pictures with Mrs Godfrey to see Julius Ceasar. Jim went to fetch her home. Arnold and George brought Paper. Dad put me five £1 certificates in War Loan.

Wednesday 14 February: Fed things. Dad, Jim and I went leading thorns from 7 acre to Rabbit Warren.

Thursday 15 February: Dad went Hedgecutting. Lilian helped me to cut and mix Mangolds. Lizzie went to keep house for Mary to let her go the Oratario, Sleaford Wes:Chapel. Walked both ways.

Friday 16 February: Dad went down Fen trying to buy Mangolds. Got truck off Mr Flintham Boys went to clean them Lizzie and Jim aft. Did little pegging morn and night.

Saturday 17 February: Dad Lizzie and I went Mangold cleaning. Put truck on 4 tons 2 cwts 25/- per ton. Harry came up

Sunday 18 February: Preacher Mr Richardson. Service at Home Speaker Lilian

Monday 19 February: Dad went to Sleaford. I did some pegging and fed things (aft) Aunt Eliza came up.

Tuesday 20 February: Rainy Day. Finished Rug. Lewis birthday (23). Jim took Taffy to go to Ruskington got to second corner turned to come home & she fell down could not get her up, think her ankle was sprained. Sent for men to Shoot Her. Poor old Taffy served us faithfully 20 yrs. We shall miss Her much and want Her often, but could not sell Her or keep Her to suffer.

Wednesday 21 February: Dad not very well. Lizzie and I went to Pouchers mangold cleaning, went in to dinner, came home 4 o'clock.

Thursday 22 February: Lizzie and I went cleaning Mangolds. Had dinner there. Boys leading them home.

Friday 23 February: Put truck Mangolds on 6 tons 3 cwts. Joey's Birthday They all came here for Tea and Supper. Going to give him framed photo of Will when it is finished.

Saturday 24 February: Cleaning stackyard up and putting stones in bad place. Dad & Jim went cleaning thorns in 7 acre. I fed things.

Sunday 25 February: Preacher Dad. I spoke aft. Service at home.

Monday 26 February: Dad went to Market. I fed things, cut front trees. Lizzie went to help Mary. Tom bought 16 acres Fen Land (Mr. Pears Dorrington) £600

Tuesday 27 February: Cleaning Stackyard up and putting stones on. Mother's Birthday 55th. Mary came to Tea. Sent to Johnsons for 1 Bushel Duke of York Seed Potatoes 14/6 & Garden Vegetable Seeds.

Wednesday 28 February: Went down Fen burning thorns & stack places (Morn) Fed things cut Chaff. Mixed Mangolds Burning Thorns 7 acre and Garden. (Aft) Dad bought Uncle Joe's Beast.

Thursday 1 March: Went cleaning thorns in far 7 acre. Dad broke his knife,[10] had to come Home. Saw Airship, Balloon and scores of Aeroplanes. Mary came wanted to buy some fowls. Lilians birthday 17th

Friday 2 March: Dad and I went down Fen, burning thorns and cutting Bush in far field. Started another Rug. Very cold and misty.

Saturday 3 March: Should have killed Pig. Man did not come. Cleaning up in stackyard. Arnold brought Papers.

Sunday 4 March: Preacher Mr Burns Miss Burns came with Him. Mr Jackson came for night, helped with service one of soldiers came Aft. I went to Chapel Morn cycled to Heckington very rough, Jim and Lilian cycled over for evening service. Very cold, came a fall of snow in the night. Lewis went to Sleaford drilling.[11]

Monday 5 March: Pegging nearly all day. Cold and Snowy. Got water boiling ready for Pig Killing Man couldn't come. Jim fetched load of water, Barrel turned over and lost it

---

[10] Hedging knife or bill hook.

[11] With army, not seed sowing

all. Had to go back for another. Lizzie went to Dorrington to see if Mr Fox would come and kill the pig.

Tuesday 6 March: Very Cold. Mr Fox came to kill Pig. Did a nice lot of pegging.

Wednesday 7 March: Rough and bitterly cold and snowy. Blew top of wheat straw over. Charlie Pattinson came to see us after being in France six months in A.V.C. Mr Fox came and cut Pig up. Finished rug.

Thursday 8 March: Very sharp frost, all waters frozen Dad went to Sale at Evedon. Made Pork pies etc. Arnold came to see if I could give Paper at Bible Class Tuesday (Dorrington C.A. Day)

Friday 9 March: Baking day. Mr Richardson came Has been ill and was taking a walk told us Arthur had got married. Luie sent the man to come and take Mother and Father's photo's—Too busy—coming again. Lewis went to Dorrington to Practice. Very sharp frost, Came on Snowy.

Saturday 10th March: Boys fetched two load Gravel & two load stone. Gravelled front paths and yard. Set row Broad Beans in Garden. Sent for parcel of Seeds from Smiths, Worcester 2/6. Mary came Lizzie did Shopping.

Sunday 11th March: Preacher Mr Dixon. Lizzie, Lilian, Jim and I went to Wes.C.A. (Night) to hear Rev. Lee Very good Service Stayed Love feast after.

Monday 12 March: Dad went to Market. Mary came to see Dad about buying fowlhouse. Mrs Will Poucher came to spend the day with us.

Tuesday 13 March: Dad & I started down Fen. Dad called to look at Mr Jeffery's Pig. I went down and cleaned grass off 9 acre road side. Mother went to Dorrington C.A. Tea. Lizzie to Service. Dad bought Pig £9-10/-

Wednesday 14 March: Went to fetch Pig home. Dad and I went to Wes.C.A. to hear Rev. Moffat Gautrey preach. Dad came Home After Tea I stayed Evening Lizzie kept House for Mary to go.

11.

Thursday 15 March: Fed things Cut Chaff for beast and horses. Mr Richardson came to Tea with Mr Lobb. Preaching Service Mr Lamyman and Miss Hammond came.

Friday 16 March: Went and finished 7 acre hedge. Sorted some of the Potatoes. Lizzie very poorly with Billiousness. Harriet came to fit Mother for her dress.

Saturday 17 March: Lizzie little better. Got up afternoon. Foal got in pond, got it out but it would not get up. Had to get Horse and Sled it Home on Gate & pull it up with pulleys. (seems alright now). Uncle Joe's and Mr Porter helped us[12]. Zepp brought down in France. Zepps out last night, 1st time since Nov. Did not hear them.

Sunday 18 March: Preacher Mr Lamyman. Soldier helped him (aft). Dad and I cycled to Kirkby Green. Only Mr Addlesee came He did not want to stay so we went back to Rowston to hear Mr Surgenor R.N.A.S. Stayed tea at Mr. Coppings. Naval boy promised to come and preach for us if He has not to go away. Mother poorly. Had to come out of Chapel.

Monday 19 March: Dad went to Market, brought Mr R. Flatters Home to look at Dollie, Changed her for their Pony and Cart. I was poorly (aft) sickness etc. Mr Grey fetched our Beast, 2 at £18 and 1 at £16 Fetched 3 from Uncle Joe's. Mother went to Harriet's to be fitted.

Tuesday 20 March: Dad had the sickness etc. don't know what's the matter with us all. I went to see if Mr Poucher could let us have a truck of Mangolds (No) Set 2 Hens Cowhovel. Very rough and Stormy for Lilian coming home.

Wednesday 21 March: A Snowy day. Lewis fetched load of mangolds. Mr Jeffrey's Sale Dad bought me lawn mower and chitting boxes.

---

[12] Sick horses are often suspended by a sling with their feet on the ground. They are more likely to die if allowed to lie down.

Thursday 22 March: Very cold, Came a lot of snow. Cut chaff for beast and horses. Dad went to Tribunal[13] to appeal for Lewis- May 1st. Sharp frost.

Friday 23 March: Dad and I went burning thorns in meadow. Photographer came & took Our Photo's Mother, Dad, then both together. Lewis alone, Dad and I together & I alone in front against big tree. Cold and Snowy Lilian trained to school. Lewis fetched maize from Stn.

Saturday 24 March: Dad and I went burning thorns in 12 acre. Set 2 Hens on Black Minorca Eggs 4/- per doz. 1 mine 1 Mary's. Lizzie & Lilian fetched Will's Photo from Sleaford. Very nice one.

Sunday 25 March: Preacher Morn Jack Baldock (aft) Mr Cook. I went to Rowston. Mr J Couling at Kirkby Green stayed Service at Rowston (Night) Lilian and Jim came.

Monday 26 March: Dad went to Market. Very rough and cold. Lilian walked Home cycle punctured Having Exam this week. Dad bought 3 rose trees.

Tuesday 27 March: Cold and Snowy. Set rose trees in front, Jim did some gardening, cut chaff Beast and Horses. Mr Flatters came & fetched harness ready to bring pony Home. Lilian took Photo orders.

Wednesday 28 March: Fed Things. I went to Billinghay to address Women's Bright Hour Lizzie went with me. Darkie's Foal 1 yr. old died.

Thursday 29 March: Circuit 2 M at Ruskingtron. Dad went I was going, had to stay Home. Sent Missionary Money £1–17–4, Our Box 8/9$^{1}/_{2}$ Mr J. Couling President Dad retiring President. Lewis took Dolly to Mr Flatters' brought Queenie back. Heifer calved, Fetched Uncle Joe He went Home again. I made a Home for calf in middle calf place. Calf came from Lincoln—9 calves to feed. Mary came to tea. Jim's Birthday 18th.

---

[13] Farmers could appeal against essential workers being conscripted for military service.

Friday 30 March: Dad, Lizzie and I went down Fen Twitching till dinner. Jim and Lizzie went back aft. Fed Things, Cut Chaff. Practice for Good Friday. Mr Silson, Couling, Edie Couling, Annie & Lucy Fixter & Naomi came.

Saturday 31 March: Down Fen Twitching Morn & setting potatoes on stack place in Milly's field. Fed Things Aft.

Sunday 1 April: Came a lot of Snow Preacher Mr J. Couling Only us there (Morn) Not Many (Aft) Mr Lunn's last Sunday, brought His books been secretary nineteen years.

Monday 2 April: Snowy Morning. Dad and Uncle Joe went to Market in Trap. I went to See Lily and the Baby. Stayed Tea came Home to milk heifer. Very Sharp frost.

Tuesday 3 April: Dad went to Ruskington. Blacksmith came to put Darkie's shoes on. Went burning thorns in Old Seeds. Lewis and I had colds and sore throats. Lilian had Tea at Mrs Godfrey's

Wednesday 4 April: Another sprinkling of snow. Dad harrowed bottom meadow with Darkie. I cleaned the Harness. Mrs Richardson brought me W. A. Money Given up. Mary, Children & Auntie Came.

Thursday 5 April: Burning thorns in Old Seeds. Fed things. Will Fixter leaving the Fen, Jess Cook going to live in their House.

Friday 6 April: Jim got His finger in Turnip Cutter. Went to Rowston to give entertainment Us, Mr and Edie Couling. Mr Silson, Tom & Naomi. Lewis had three hours drilling made him late. Dad, Mother, Lilian went in trap. Lizzie and I stayed to do the work. I rode home in trap, Lilian my cycle. Went off well. Auntie came to stay with G.Mother.

Saturday 7 April: Drilling 4 acre Barley (New Seed) far end Charlie's field. Cut Chaff for Uncle Joe. Mr Wortley came.

Sunday 8 April: Went to Ruskington S.S.A. morn. Preacher Rev. A. Wortley. Dad & I went to Mary's dinner Lizzie to

Cutler's. I cycled to Dunston for C.A. Had tea at Lucy's. Mother with Miss Semper. Very rough coming home could not ride all the way. Summer time begins 2 am.

Monday 9 April: Snow & Thunder storms Bitterly cold. Jim took Water Cart to have New Tap in. Dad, Lilian and I went to Sleaford. Lilian had tooth drawn. Dad bought Mary fowl run. Mr Wortley came to Tea. We all went to hear Him lecture on "Confessions of a Minister" Very Good, I had to play for them, Bessie gone away.

Tuesday 10 April: Frosty and Snowy Morning. Cut Chaff, Lewis cut His finger on Chaff cutter knife. Dad fetched Paper. Mr Lunn's left the Fen. Gone to Rauceby, been in the Fen all the time we have. Shall miss Him at Chapel.

Wednesday 11 April: Snowy Morning, cleaned up. Went down Fen & drilled $2^1/_2$ acres Barley (Standwell) in far 9 Acre next to Tom's. Lilian went to school, pipes burst. Went to Mrs Godrey's for lesson. Lizzie went twitching aft. Came on Snow again.

Thursday 12 April: Been a lot of rain could not get on land. Lewis fetched qr[14] Peas from Stn. Set row Potatoes Golden Wonder & two rows of Peas in my garden & Onion Seed. (Very Wet) Lizzies Birthday.

Friday 13 April: Been some more rain cut Chaff. Went down Fen 11 o'clock Lizzie and I stayed till 6 o'clock. Jim came down aft. Mary came.

Saturday 14 April: Went down Fen twitching. Wet and Stormy. Dad went to Anwick. Harry came.

Sunday 15 April: Started Sunday School & Evening Service. C.A. Preacher Mrs Shaw Chapel full (aft) Mrs Phillips and Children came to Tea. Mary and Arnold for Night Service.

Monday 16 April: Dad went to Market. Lizzie, I & Mrs Start went twitching[15] came on rain Had to leave it. Cut chaff

---

[14] Two large sacks approximately $^1/_4$ ton in total weight.

[15] Twitch is the local name for Couch Grass, a pernicious weed which was almost impossible to control before chemical weedkillers were evolved.

for Horses and Beast. Lucy came for Lesson. Lilian started Sleaford School again New Teacher (Miss Swan)

Tuesday 17 April: Bitterly Cold. Went Twitching did not go very well. Rainy & Snowy first off. I went back (aft). Lilian went to Sleaford & to Mrs Godfrey's. Lewis went to Leasingham Dorrington Choir giving Entertainment. Lizzie washed.

Wednesday 18 April: Wet Morning. Did not go down Fen. C.A.Tea 5 & 5.30 I stayed with grandmother. Entertainment did not go off real well, Mr Lobb Chairman. Mr Alex. W. Surgenor spoke. (from Cranwell) He, Mr Lobb, Annie, stayed overnight. Had nice talk about Aeroplanes went to bed 1.30.

Thursday 19 April: Down Fen twitching Lizzie and I stayed till 6 o'clock, real tired.

Friday 20 April: Down Fen twitching, Mrs Start helping us, first fine night & day. Mr King came for the day, with their Motor trolley going to Skegness. Lilian at School and Mrs Godfrey's.

Saturday 21 April: Down Fen twitching Mrs Start came again. Not such a nice day though did not rain much. Turned three beast out daytime.

Sunday 22 April: Preacher Mr Lobb. I was planned Ruskington morn. Mr Lobb came. Came Home dinner with me went to Mr Phillips to Tea. Lizzie went to Sleaford S.S.A. Morn.

Monday 23 April: Very busy day dragged part of 1st 9 acre. Heavy, Light and chain Harrowed 4 acre drilled 2 acre Oats in Charlie's field (roadside). I Harrowed after drill. Mrs Start and Lizzie burning twitch, I helped among came Home five o'clock. Cut Chaff fed Things. Cleaned two drills out Ours and Wrights. Gave Lucy lesson. Mother went to Ruskington to see Mrs Codd. Mary's Birthday 33rd.

Tuesday 24th April: Drilled $5^1/_2$ acres Barley in 1st 9 acre and 2 acre in Charlie's field I Harrowed with Bob. Heavy day but glad to get it in. Mrs Start and Lizzie burning twitch. Sent to Newbury's for new dress.

Wednesday 25 April: Cleaning up and burning thorns. Fed things, Turned Cows out. Washed and Churned.

Thursday 26 April: Drilled 2 acre Peas in 12 acre. some in Old Seeds[16] & some Tares. Getting Potatoes out of Grave, some frozen. Airship came down in Mr. Wright's field (Washdyke) Gardening set 15 different kinds of seeds

Friday 27 April: I went down Fen Harrowed $5^1/_2$ acres in 9 acre Barley & part of the Oats. Mr Lobb came to Tea. Started Band of Hope Meetings, 21 present, a very nice meeting. Lilian's 1st day Exam (Sleaford) Mrs Godfrey's to Tea.

Saturday 28 April: Went burning twitch in 1st 9 acre then to far 9 acre to get ready for Carotts. Dad went to Billinghay to see for the drill. Lilian's 2nd day Exam.

Sunday 29 April: School Morn. 1st Practice for S.S.A. Preacher at Home Tom. I at Leasingham Very rough going. Mary and Children came. My Birthday 33rd. also Mr Coppings, Mrs Smith Sharpes, Mrs T.E. Richardsons, Mrs Dixons (Leasingham) & little Bobbies.

Monday 30 April: Went down Fen to get ready for drilling Carrotts. Lewis went for drill 11.30 got it 2.30 made us late. drilled 2 acre Carrotts. Dad came Home to go to Market.

Tuesday 1 May: Went down Fen cleaning twitch and digging corners. Cut Chaff.

Wednesday 2 May: Took 8 beast to Ruskington. Went to drill a bit of Barley for Uncle Joe. I went down Fen to Roll while Jim finished some Harrowing. Mrs Tory & Keyworth came to see me about the W.A. they are starting off again Mrs Tory Secretary Mrs Phillips Treasurer. Had their money back again.

Thursday 3 May: My Byke punctured front wheel yesterday

---

[16] Old Seeds is the name of a field: it was probably used as temporary pasture and had recently been ploughed up.

back wheel today ran over a smashed up glass bottle. Went down Fen digging back of shed.

Friday 4 May: Went down Fen started to dig back of the shed then had to go twitching in far field. Cut chaff. Band of Hope Meeting, Henry Leader, David Reader, Girls sang & Henry read a Poem.

Saturday 5 May: Down Fen, finished garden back of shed, down in far field twitching and getting potatoes out.

Sunday 6 May: School Morn 1st Practice for S.S.A. Preacher Richie.

Monday 7 May: Got Potatoes out of 12 acre. Helped Dad get ready for Market. Went down Fen and burnt crop of twitch off little field. Got Potatoes out of grave in Fen.

Tuesday 8 May: Setting Potatoes in far field, I, Lizzie, Joey, Maggie Kirk, Mrs. Cook & Tyle. I set some then helped Dad to cut and fetch some more, left 3 rows short of Potatoes, got home 6.30. Dad's byke punctured soon as He started went on mine. Lucy came for lesson. (Very Tired) Mr Dixon brought me a Solo to play for Him.

Wednesday 9 May: Dad & I went down Fen in far 9 acre twitching. Lizzie washed & Churned. Tom came to little Pigs for Dad. Mr Dixon called. Finished my Garden, Finished Dad's Garden - (Jim done it)

Thursday 10 May: Lizzie & I set 36 rows of potatoes for Mr Harpham for lending us the plough, finished setting ours in little field 12 st. from Mr William Phillips. Practice at Chapel for S.S.A.

Friday 11 May: Went down Fen in far 9 acre twitching. I rolled the carrot land Took Aunt Eliza's Shoes down. Cut front lawn, Lizzie went to Mary's. Lilian to Billinghay for Shoes.

Saturday 12 May: I went & finished Harrowing far 7 acre wheat. Took Darkie 17 down Fen. Dad, Lizzie and Lilian getting Mangold land ready. Lizzie & I stayed twitching, Jim pushoeing Carrot land

Sunday 13 May: Came a severe thunderstorm last night about 12. Practice Morn Lilian & I went to Kirkby Green (aft) Lilian to play 6 present beside us. Miss Poucher played at Home. Preacher Mr J.Couling Mr Dixon came in to play Jim's Solo. Harriet came, Miss Hammond & Drucie came in. Very Hot.

Monday 14 May: Went down Fen twitching burning. Came Home and went to Market, Lewis Having His holiday, went to Sleaford.

Tuesday 15 May: Dad went to fetch drill from Ravell's Shed drilled 9 acre small seeds in Old Seeds. Lizzie Harrowed with Bob, Jim had Violet and Darkie[17] down Fen. Came on Cold & Stormy.

Wednesday 16 May: Very Cold Went down Fen. Dad took drill home with Darkie I light Harrowed with Darkie.

Thursday 17 May: Went down Fen twitching in far 9 acre. Cut Chaff (aft). Came on rain.

Friday 18 May: Dad, Lizzie & I went twitching been lot of rain and it was wet. Set Kidney Beans. Practice at Chapel. Mr Dixon came. Lewis came back from Newark went up North Hills. Rained a little.

Saturday 19 May: Down Fen getting ready for Mangolds. Came on Stormy. Got ready to go to Broughton S.S.A.. Lizzie & Lena went to Old Roman Road. with me, I went from there in $^1/_2$ hr. Came on rain.

Sunday 20 May: School to Hear Recitations Morn. Children's Service aft. I preached at night. Mrs Tindal and Mrs Freeman were called out to a man who had died, missed them at chapel. Uncle Charlie came walked a little way home with Him. Our chapel closed. Dad, Lilian, Lewis, Jim went Dorrington. Mother Anwick, Lizzie Dorrington aft. & night. Mother stayed home night.

Monday 21 May: Emily & I went to Mrs Winter's to fetch Butter for Tea. Then to Chapel to cut up. Went to Sing round

---

[17] Bob, Violet, and Darkie are the names of the farm horses.

the Village 2 to 4 o'clock 30/-. Tea for Scholars & teachers No Public Tea. Meeting at 7 o'clock Chairman Mr H. Kennewell I gave an address Mr Lobb ill, could not come.

Tuesday 22 May: Came Home arrived 10 to 9 o'clock. Went down Fen to help to drill mangolds Drilled $5^1/_2$ acres. Dad let the soldiers go pushoeing 6d an hr.

Wednesday 23 May: Zepps were out last night, got warning Ruskington. Went down Fen Harrowing with Bob in first 9 acre. Dad & Mother went to Mr Lunn's Funeral (Ruskington) Dorrington S.S.A. Mother and Lizzie went. Mr Baldock came for some eggs. Lena went to Horbling, going to Nottingham tomorrow.

Thursday 24 May: Stormy Morning. Dad & I ploughed and set mangold grave with potatoes. Took 3 beast to Ruskington. Mother, I, Lilian & Jim went to Ruskington C.A. Gentlemen's Entertainment. 12 Solos, Jim said two Recitations.

Friday 25 May: I went down Fen rolled carrott and mangold land with Darkie. Boys Horsehoed 1st 9 acre barley. Practice at Chapel.

Saturday 26 May: I went down Fen twitching Boys Horsehoeing in Charlie's Field. Dad & I took His Byke to Bratleys[18] went to Stn to meet Mrs King did not see Her, came to Mary's & found Her there Mr King came in Motor.

Sunday 27 May: Practice Morn. Dad, Mrs King and I went to Kirkby Green Mrs K. took Service for Dad I played came Home through Scopwick. Preacher at Home Mr Evans.

Monday 28 May: Lizzie & I went down Fen forking twitch in 1st 9 acre. Mr & Mrs King went with Dad to Market. Marys came.

Tuesday 29 May: Stormy Morning (Thundered) Boys went to Plough fallows in 12 acre aft. I went hoeing in Peas. Dad

---

[18] Bratleys was a large ironmongers in the Market Place, Sleaford.

20.

took Mother to Sleaford to look at firegrate. Shops closed. Miss Cunningtons & company came.

Wednesday 30 May: I went to lead horses for Lewis hosehoeing in Milly's field & Peas. Dad & Jim pushoeing Carrotts. Practice at Chapel for Children.

Thursday 31 May: Jim started to cycle Home to Hull 7.30. I helped Dad to finish Pushoeing the Carrotts. Went in Peas aft.

Friday 1 June: Lizzie rolled Mangold land with Darkie. Dad & I twitching in 1st 9 acre. Practice at Chapel Jack & Bessie.

Saturday 2 June: Dad, Lizzie & I hoeing in Peas. Lilian had P.C. to say Jim arrived Home 2.15. Dad & Mother went to look at new Grate for Kitchen took Mr & Mrs King to meet 6.30 train for Home. George and Ruth rode with them, Mary and Arnold Home with them.

Sunday 3 June: Practice Morn. Preacher Mr Smith Dad planned Ruskington (Eve) I went with took first part of Service. Jack & Flo walked up with us

Monday 4 June: Dad & Lewis ploughing all day Lizzie & I went in Peas Morn I took dinner down Fen went hoeing Barley in first 9 acre. Cut side lawn.

Tuesday 5 June: Dad fetched some Coal. Lizzie helped Mother to clean Pantry went in Peas night. I went in Carrotts Dad came to help me. Practice for Children. Bratleys brought Dad's Byke.

Wednesday 6 June: Getting swede land ready. Lizzie came home fetched dinner so that we could burn twitch off. Did Gravel paths night.

Thursday 7 June: Lizzie washed, Getting swede land ready, Rainy morning Mr Lobb came for Dinner from Heckington Dad & I came home dinner. Mr Cook got as far as our house with wagon load straw, overturned the waggon in the gateway. helped him load and get it up. Clothes line broke with curtains etc. Dad & Mr Lobb drove to

Billinghay. Band of Hope Meeting, 35 present Children were Choir Mr Lobb gave an address. Signed our cards got 9 new adult members 36 altogether, Coll 7/- very good throughout.

Friday 8 June: Getting Swede land ready Lizzie brought dinner. Went in Carrots aft. Dads byke punctured, Practice at Chapel. Auntie and Annie Cunnington came up.

Saturday 9 June: Drilled Swedes (3 acres) Mr Cook rolled for us & we drilled 1 acre for Him. I Harrowed after the drill. Lizzie & I went in Carrotts (aft). Mended Dad's byke.

Sunday 10 June: Mr Hewerdine came to fetch me to go to Wilsford S.S.A. Got ready and went back with Him 9.30. Mr Shaw planned (missed Her train Sat night) We caught Her up (driving over) near to Wilsford. Stayed & helped Her with Services. Lizzie came to meet me, Got mile out of Sleaford.

Monday 11 June: My byke punctured picked up a piece of Glass last night. Mended it & Dad's. Dad went to Ruskington. His byke burst & He sent it to Sleaford for new tube. Lizzie & I went in Carrotts, Dad came aft. Practice at Chapel.

Tuesday 12 June: Dad & I in Carrotts. Lizzie rolling Mangold land Came home brought us some Tea. Stayed till 9 o'clock.

Wednesday 13 June: Carrott weeding Mrs Vintner came to help, Lizzie stayed Home to wash Annie Cunnington came voluntarily to help We stayed till 6 o-clock. Went in my garden. —

Thursday 14 June: Phillipps let us have His five women to help in Carrotts 10 of us altogether. Mrs Harrod & Mrs Vintner helped us. Lilian brought tea to barn. Cleaned it and put platform up, Practice Children.

Friday 15 June: Lizzie poorly Annie went in Carrotts, Mrs Harrod came Mrs Vintner didn't come. Practice at barn— Worst we've had.

Saturday 16 June: Annie & Dad & I Carrotting called at barn to finish up. Dad & I went to meet Mr Bromage by 6.40 train. Had very bad cold.

Sunday 17 June: Service Morn Chapel full Beautiful Service. Lilian recited an appeal for S. School. Aft. Children did well (Organ went wrong 1st hymn it was dreadful. Started 2nd hymn without it) Mr Dixon put it right. Barn packed. Thundered all the night stopped some from coming to Service, rained a little when we came Home A very good day Morn 16/- Aft 44/- Eve 27/3. 22 to Tea. Mr Lobb planned. He & Annie came for the day. Pony went twice each time.

Monday 18 June: Lizzie & I went down Fen weeding Carrotts Mr Vintner came Mrs Cook & Mrs Harrod did not come. Came Home 3 o'clock to say Goodbye to Mr Bromage went Home by the 4.30 Sorry He could not stay. Marys came.

Tuesday 19 June: Went weeding Carrotts Mrs Harrod came nearly finished them. Cut seeds in Baldock's field & an acre for Mr Cook. Dad's byke burst walked home I mended it.

Wednesday 20 June: Not very Well stayed in Bed. Mother got her finger in mangel Had to get up & make butter up. Mother went to Dr. to Have Her finger dressed. S.S.A. I had to stay Home to milk. Lilian helped Mother went down early. Miss Hammond, Annie Fixter, Mrs Cook & Mrs Poucher helping & Lizzie. Children had Tea on Grass. I went for 3rd Sitting. Service Mr Copping Chairman few recitations. Mr Lobb gave an address. Not quite so many to Tea or Service, but total £8-10/- nearly, about 8/- up from last year.

Thursday 21 June: Went and cleaned Barn. Dad & I went to the L.M. (Rowston) took Richie with us. No one else came but Mr J. Couling (President) & Jack Baldock (Aft) Nice day Came Home to Milk came a lovely rain set 66 plants out in my garden.

Friday 22 June: Dad & I chopping Mangolds out. Mrs Vintner finished Carrotts. Lizzie went hoeing in garden. Wrote to Mrs Bromage.

Saturday 23 June: Lizzie not well. Came down Fen aft. Dad & I chopping Mangolds out. Lewis scuffling Potatoes, Mrs Vintner did not come. Lizzie and Lilian went to Leasingham to Practice.

Sunday 24 June: Dad & I went to School morn. Lewis, Lizzie, Lilian & Jim went to Leasingham S.S.A. for the day. Preacher at Home Mr G.A.,Couling. I was planned Meth. Fen. Dad drove me. Got to Ruskington, Poured with Rain, Called at Toms Had Tea Set off again. Rained hard all the way there 10 present a little late getting there. Fine coming Home.

Monday 25 June: Fetched Truck Coal 9 tons. Mother poorly, Lizzie stayed Home till dinner. Turning seeds aft did not quite finish. Mary came Miss Ambler called, lost Annie Cock Had gone in 7 acre.

Tuesday 26 June: Chopping Mangolds out Lizzie washed I wasn't well, little better aft. Lilian & Jim went to Leasingham S.S.A.

Wednesday 27 June: Went in Mangolds till lunch then in Seeds, Started leading (Aft) Got 7 load to the Shed place.

Thursday 28 June: Wet Morn went in Potatoes (aft) did 28 rows.

Friday 29 June: Wet morn went in Pototoes (aft) did 28 rows.

Saturday 30 June: Dad poorly Lizzie & I turned seeds, Boys came dinner time and we finished leading them. Lilian came to tell us Dad wasn't coming down & Mother was going to Newark, Had a letter to say Aunt S.J. Husband had died. Mother went 6.30 train to Mrs Johnson's. Going Syerston tomorrow.

Sunday 1 July: School Morn, Preacher planned Dad Mr Dixon changed Him & He came. J. Poucher came to Tea.

Monday 2 July: Dad & I went Hoeing Potatoes. Came Home dinner drove into Sleaford. Lewis went to the Funeral.

24.

Mother & Lewis came Home, Lewis cycled, Mother came last Train.

Tuesday 3 July: All went Hoeing Potatoes Finished them. Marys came then Mr Squire & Emmie, then Miss Cunnington, then Uncle Joe.

Wednesday 4 July: Finished Chopping Mangolds out. Lewis Topped His stack up. Dad & I went in Carrotts Aft. Lizzie & Mrs Vintner Singling Mangolds

Thursday 5 July: I went Hoeing Carrotts. Lizzie and Mrs Vintner in Mangolds Dad came down, Went Home again. Lizzie, Lilian and I went pulling docks in Beans (12 acre) night.

Friday 6 July: I went Hoeing Mangolds. Lizzie & Mrs V. in Mangolds. Dad not well came down Aft. Lewis Hilled Potatoes. Lizzie, Lilian & I went docking night.

Saturday 7 July: I went in Carrotts. Lizzie & Mrs V. in Mangolds. Mr Lamyman came to chop Swedes out. Dad, I, Lewis & Jim went & led Mrs Start's Hay for Her. Dad little better. S.S. Hy.Bks. came.

Sunday 8 July: School morn. Started with new S.S.Hymn books. I went to Heckington (Cycled). Preacher planned Mr Dixon, Charlie Cutler took Aft. for Dad, Harry night. Mary and Children came to Tea. George stayed all night.

Monday 9 July: Dad & Mother went to Market. I went Hoeing Carrotts, Lizzie in Mangolds. Dad, Lizzie, Lilian & I went docking.

Tuesday 10 July: I went in Carrotts. Mr Lamyman started in Swedes. Very sharp frost cut all the Potatoes off. Went & Finished docking in beans Jim went with us.

Wednesday 11 July: I went in Carrotts, Dad stayed Home. Mr Lamyman in Swedes. Drucie came for a practice.

Thursday 12 July: I went in Carrotts till dinner. Dad fetched New Grate from Bratley's. I went to look at our Potatoes they were not damaged much, Came Home dinner Started leading Hay. B. of Hope, Lewis & Naomi got it up, Minister came 8 new members Coll 3/5$^{1}/_{2}$.

Friday 13 July: Mr Silson put new grate in, Dad helped Mr Silson. Leading Hay I raked & helped on the stack. Lewis went to drill I stacked last two loads. Soldiers started to Hoe beans in 12 acre.

Saturday 14 July: I went in Carrotts. Cut Fen lane, Road & 1st 9 & far 9 acre bank. Paid Mrs Vintner off. Mrs. Richardson came see about Picnic. Lilian fetched some Rhubarb from Mrs G. Peatmans. I got some Rasps. Peas & Potatoes from my Garden. Lilian & Jim some Peas from 12 acre.

Sunday 15 July: School morn. Thundered aft not many at Chapel Preacher planned Charlie Cutler Dad should have taken aft. I took it for Him. Charlie came for night Chapel full 53. Drucie and Alice came for a practice.

Monday 16 July: I Heaped grass in lane then went in carrotts. Lizzie stayed Home to wash. Jim mowing dykes Lewis scuffling Swedes. Had meeting about B. of Hope Anniversary Decided to have Picnic give invitation to Ruskington & Dorrington Meet at 2. Service at 3 to 4 Chairman Minister Speakers Sister Hope & Lieut. Col.[19] Murray Games aft Tea. No prizes.

Tuesday 17 July: Hoeing Mangolds.

Wednesday 18 July: Wet day. I took Pony to Sleaford for some Cartridges. A Beautiful rain wanted it badly, no water excepting pond across meadow. Lilian & Jim went to Practice. Mother, Lizzie & Dad drove to Dorrington to see Tom. Cooked Peas & New Potatoes for Sleaford:

Thursday 19 July: Hoeing Mangolds. Richie came to see about Picnic.

Friday 20 July: Hoeing Mangolds. Three men killed at Cranwell Airship got away, they had hold of ropes fell and were killed.[20]

Saturday 21 July: Finished Mangolds. Mr Bell brought

---

[19] Brigadier Murray had been promoted to Lieut. Colonel in April 1917. (Salvation Army rank sequence is not the same as in the British Army.)

[20] A Submarine Scout airship being placed in a hangar was caught by a gust of wind and carried aloft.

G.Mother Home. Lizzie went to Sleaford with Lamp.

Sunday 22 July: School Morn. New Plans came. I went to Dorrington Preacher at Home Mr Gant for Mrs Shaw.

Monday 23 July: Dad & I went Hoeing Swedes till dinner then to market. Boys Scuffling Mangolds Lizzie washed. Com.Mtg. for Picnic Mr Richie. W.Kelley, W.Wilcox, Miss Cutler & Scott from Ruskington us & Naomi.

Tuesday 24 July: Dad, Lizzie & I hoeing Carrotts. Mr Lamyman and Boys in the Swedes. Had some New Potatoes & Green Peas out of my Garden for Supper.

Wednesday 25 July: Dad, Lizzie & I hoeing Carrotts. Lewis cleaning Pond out. Dad, Lewis & Jim went to fence beast out at Ruskington. Lilian & Jim went for B.of H. Practice at Ruskington.

Thursday 26 July: Dad, Lizzie and I in Carrotts. Had to start carting water for all the stock.

Friday 27 July: Dad stayed Home to help lead water, Lizzie and I finished Carrotts. Lilian Broke up at Ruskington School. Came a Heavy storm in the evening & drifted one of the airships close past, we were afraid as they couldn't control it, came down just behind Haverholme wood. No one hurt.

Saturday 28 July: Hoeing Swedes, Dad, Lizzie, I, Jim & Mr. Lamyman. Had last lot of Peas out of my Garden. Five Suppers from them. Lewis went to Harrowby to Camp.

Sunday 29 July: Dad & L:izzie went to hear Mr Harper for Con. Sunday, He did not come, Mr Squire preached. I went to School then to Leasingham. Preacher at Home Mr Burns & Mr Jackson.

Monday 30 July: Lilian had to go to Sleaford School. Dad & I went to Market rained and did not put by came Home Leasingham way. Went to Rowston to see Mr Lobb about B. of Hope.

Tuesday 31 July: Mowing thistles in Grass field. Mended Pond sides with bricks etc. Cold and stormy. Lewis came Home from Camp.

Wednesday 1 August: Wet day. Helped in house. Mr Murray came for His Holiday 6.30 train.

Thursday 2 August: Wet morning. Cleaned traphouse. Mr Lobb came, Band of Hope (Lilian & Jim) Jim led, Mr Lobb sang, Mr Murray spoke, 6 new members making 50.

Friday 3 August: Wet most of the day, Spudding Thistles in grass field morn. Cleaning front aft. Dad & Mr Murray went for a drive. Lilian walked into Sleaford took cycle to have Chain mended. Broke up noon.

Saturday 4 August: I went in Swedes (Morn). Dad & Mr Murray met Mr & Mrs Hoyes from Sleaford 10 o'clock. Dad & I met Sister Hope & Madge 4.30 Lewis slept North Hills, Lilian in Parlour.

Sunday 5 August: Mr Murray, Jim, Lizzie, Madge, Mr & Mrs Hoyes went to Ruskington morn. Sister Hope & Mr Lobb to school both spoke to Children. Band of Hope Anniversary, Preacher Mr Lobb, Children in Choir sang Water from heaven, Drucie sang solo, Lead me to Jesus. Coll. $8/2^1/_2$, 13/-. Lilian played aft. I evening.

Monday 6 August: Lobb, Annie & Mrs Copping came dinner. Band of Hope Anniversary. Getting ready morn. Picnic Rusk Fen. Rusk. & Dorrington arrived 1.30. Service 3. Mr Lobb presided. Speakers Mr Murray & Sister Hope. Coll. 27/6 Tea on Grass & games after. A Beautiful Day 156 Members Tickets sold. I made Paper flowers for Prizes 1st. Blue 2nd. Yellow 3rd. Green, finished up 9 o'clock. We went to meet waggon to ride back.

Tuesday 7 August: Dad & Mr Murray took Sister Hope & Madge to Rowston. They stayed overnight. Drove Mr & Mrs Hoyes & Mother to Roxholm.

Wednesday 8 August: I went down Fen Heaping grass. Sister Hope & Madge came back 11.20. They, Dad. Lewis, I, Mr Murray, Mr Hoyes & Lilian went down Fen in Waggon rode Home on the Hay. Mr & Mrs Hoyes went Home by 6.20 from Here. Jim mowing Peas.

Thursday 9 August: Damp morning. Dad took Mr Murray,

Sister Hope & Madge to Sleaford round by Heckington Home. I set 170 plants in Garden.

Friday 10 August: Boys finished Peas. Opened 1st. 7 acre Oats & 7 acre Wheat. Sister & Madge went to Cutler's to Tea Lizzie & I fetched them Home. They went to Couling's Waterworks morn.[21]

Saturday 11 August: Mr Murray went Home 11.20. Been shower Started Binding Oats Came storm aft. Only got half done. Mary came. Jim & Sister Hope met Mr Cushing 4.30. Lizzie, I, Sister & Madge fetched 4 cans water Mr C. went with us.

Sunday 12 August: Sister Hope went with me to school, the others to Ruskington. Preacher Rev. E. Cushing, two very good Services. Came a Heavy thunderstorm tea time spoilt Congregation. Colls. $9/0^1/_2$.

Monday 13 August: Mr Cushing went Home 8 train. Mr Lobb started to cycle Home 310 miles[22]. Dad, Sister, Madge, Lilian & I went to Market. Sister, Madge & I stayed Tea (Mary's) Lizzie came. Committee Mtg. to settle up for Picnic, very satisfactory.

Tuesday 14 August: Started pulling beans 6 acre in twelve acre, very short. Sister Hope went to see Mrs Hale Dunston Madge to Mary's. Reaped a few more Oats.

Wednesday 15 August: Finished cutting Oats. Started 7 acre Wheat, Stormy. Lizzie Sister, Madge & I went down to Uncle's.

Thursday 16 August: Finished 7 acre Wheat. Sister Hope & Madge went Home 11.20. Went to cut 7 acre wheat in Walked foot path for Uncle Joe, Lizzie turned Peas, Lilian & I pulling beans, Jim opened Old Seeds.

Friday 17 August: Finished Cutting Uncle's wheat. Went five rounds in Old Seeds. Lizzie & Jim went mowing and tying laid Wheat in Milly's field, Lilian took dinner, came

---

[21] By the roadside in Dorrington Fen

[22] A reasonable supposition for 1917 would be that he went part (probably most) of the journey by train taking his cycle with him. [See entry for 9th Sept.]

Home Tea. Went pulling beans. Stormy day.

Saturday 18 August: Cutting wheat in Old Seeds 8 acre. Came storm aft. but finished 5 o'clock. Harry came up.

Sunday 19 August: School morn. Dad planned Kirkby Green, I at Rowston, cycled. Stayed Eve. Service. Mr Redding took Service for me. Preacher at Home C. Addlesee

Monday 20 August: Cut half Milly's field wheat & started Oats in Charlie's field.

Tuesday 21 August: Cut middle 2 acre Barley in Charlie's field, finished Oats & started far 4 acre Barley. Jim opened out far 9 acre. Shelled my Peas, cut cress & got kidney beans. Mended Lizzie's Byke.

Wednesday 22 August: Lizzie went tying Barley in far 9 acre. Boys finished Cutting Charlie's field & far 9 acre (2 acres) Dad, Lilian, & I led & stacked Peas & 2 load of wheat from 1st. 7 acre. I went to meet Lilian with tins for some water.

Thursday 23 August: Damp morning, Lewis raked Pea land. Dad, Jim & I went stouking far 9 acres & opening out 1st 9 acre . Started reaping aft. Came Thunderstorm had to stop. Went in beans after Tea.

Friday 24 August: Cut other half Milly's field Wheat. Then in 9 acre Barley did not quite finish, Lizzie, Lilian, Jim stouked Oats & Barley in Charlie's field. Very rough and hard work.

Saturday 25 August: Finished Cutting Barley brought binder home put it away. Jim, Lilian & Lizzie stouked far 9 acre barley then help me with 1ˢᵗ 9 acre Dad went with Harry to Sleaford. Leading 7 acre wheat Harry helping us.

Sunday 26 August: School morn, Sister Hope sent some tickets, called all old ones in. Lizzie went with me to Kirkby Green aft. Preacher Emmie Cutler. Came on rain.

Monday 27 August: Been a lot of rain in the night. All went bean pulling. Grandmother fell down Arnold fetched Dad and Lilian Home.

Tuesday 28 August: Rained all night. Mended fowl House put

fowls in. Dad & Jim took three beast to Ruskington, brought Heifer Home. Went pulling beans Boys tying Came on rain aft Dinner came home without finishing them. G.mother little better.

Wednesday 29 August: Damp morning, Led Old Seeds field wheat, finished 7 acre & rakings Dad & I went down Fen finished stouking wheat went to look at potatoes (morn).

Thursday 30 August: Led 2 acre wheat in Twelve acres. Jim raked Old Seeds & 2 acre & we fetched them home. Went down Fen for three load wheat out of Milly's field, Dad went to Sale (Pattinson's) 3 o'clock bought Mrs Start's place. £330.[23]

Friday 31 August: Damp Morning been lots of Rain. Boys went to plough in Old Seeds (Morn) Dad, Lillian & I in beans till dinner. Then Lizzie gathered & tied swathe in Charlie's field. Dad & I in both 9 acres. Got 3 load wheat out Milly's field. Violet's load weighed her up.

Saturday 1 September: Lot of rain in the night. Boys went to plough. Dad, Lizzie, Lilian & I finished pulling. Tying & stouking Beans. Mother & Dad went for a ride Aft. Came on rain, Lizzie to Tea at Mary's.

Sunday 2 September: School morn. Preacher Mr Hewerdine. Jim planned Kirkby Green.

Monday 3 September: Went down Fen for 2 load Wheat. Led, Raked & Cleared 1st 7 acre Oats. Went down Fen for 5 load Oats from Charlie's field. A grand day after all stormy weather. Everybody hard at work.

Tuesday 4 September: Jim fetched Bob. Pattinson's Cart rave broke Jim took it to Rusk. Got it mended. Fetched 4 loads Oats, 8 load Barley from far 9 acre. 4 Carts.

Wednesday 5 September: Finished far 9 acre Barley. Started 1st 9 acre.

Thursday 6 September: Auntie Cunnington came home from Holiday.

---

[23] The Agricultural Returns for the previous year, 1916, show that John Start was the occupant of Hillside Farm which had an area of 181 acres.

Friday 7 September: Led Beans. Then started leading Barley from Charlie's field 14 load home.

Saturday 8 September: Finished leading Charlie's field. Raked part of Millie's field. Got all sheaves Home only Fen rakings left. Harry helped (aft) a beautiful fine week. Mr Murray sent Mother Biscuit Barrel. Jim went to Lincoln to see his Father & Mother.

Sunday 9 September: School Morn. I went to Heckington Dad to Dorrington to Preacher. Mr Lobb at Ruskington Home from His holiday Trained to Leicester cycled Home. Lilian & Lizzie went to Practice Ruskington. Preacher at Home Mr W. Kelly (aft) Mr Wainer (Eve)

Monday 10 September: Jim arrived back 7 o'clock. Lewis went to cut 2nd Crop of clover in Baldock's field Reaper wouldn't work. Borrowed Mr Kirk's. Jim went Horseraking He & Lewis fetched 2 load Rakings Home. made them late. Lizzie went heaping rakings morn. Dad & I fetched rakings from Millie's field then went to Market called for Mrs Murray 4.30 train did not come till 6.30 Dad and Lizzie met the train. Lilian started school.

Tuesday 11 September: Manure carting to far 7 acre. Soldier helping us. I was driving middle carts. Dad, Mrs Murray & I went for a drive to see Mr Cole about thrashing then on to Cranwell.[24] Sentry let us through had good look around about 2 hours. saw all over the Camp just right for the evening flight saw nearly 100 aeroplanes Oh what a buzz did enjoy it everything was beautifully kept. Did not see the man & have to go again. Saw airship come down & go up.

Wednesday 12 September: Manure Carting Soldier helping us. Fetched barley rakings from Charlie's field. Harvest Home.

Thursday 13 September: Manure Carting Soldier helping. Dug

---

[24] The R.N.A.S. Central Training Establishment, part of H.M.S. Daedalus opened 1/4/16. All Royal Naval personnel under instruction in aeroplanes, seaplanes, balloons, and airships were sent here.

early Potatoes in garden. Mrs Murray went Home 11.20

Friday 14 September: Manure Carting morn. Dad & I went down to look at Clover. Came Home all went down Horseraked Heaped & brought four load home. Soldier helping us.

Saturday 15 September: Dad, Lizzie Lilian & I cycled to Lincoln started 9am. a fair breeze side front. My front tube burst at Blankney like a gun. Lilian took it on to Metheringham I walked on Lilian & Lizzie rode round to Nocton Miss Semper gone to Lincoln, Got new tube 6/- Met them on Top road, Arrived Lincoln 12am. Got rewards, Lilian blouse & Dress went to Cathedral & Arbouretum started Home 5 o'clock arrived 7pm rather tired

Sunday 16 September: School morn Gave out rewards. I cycled to Dunston, only 5 (aft). Went to Lucy's to Tea found her brighter than I expected. Had to have lamps coming Home.

Monday 17 September: Put clocks back 1 hr. Old time. Finished Manure Carting. Harry took first few loads. Dad, Lizzie & I went to Market took 150 eggs 30/-. I bought new Hat 17/5 Lizzie blouse 9/11, went round to Scotchman's then to Farmer Wright's for Sugar. 1 st. come instead of 4st. Auntie Cunnington, Her Friend & Phil came

Tuesday 18 September: Dad & I took 4 calves to Ruskington. Then down Fen to Kirk's, Bought sample Carrotts took them to Cranwell sold 1 ton @ £4 per ton to deliver them. Came on rain.

Wednesday 19 September: Wet morning mended Bags, Bycycle etc. Dad, Jim, Lizzie & I went and got 1 ton Carrotts in bags aft. Lewis fetched them home. Lizzie & Lilian went to practice.

Thursday 20 September: Lewis took Carrotts to Cranwell. Got Plums, Damcenes from Garden. Altered my Grey dress.

Friday 21 September: Getting Potatoes up in Garden. Started making Shed in corner of Crewyard. Mother went to Mary's Jim & Lilian fetched Her Home.

Saturday 22 September: Getting potatoes up in Garden. Making Shed in Crewyard. Expecting Mr and Mrs Godfrey, did not come.

Sunday 23 September: Wet morn. Ruskington H.F. Dad went Morn. Lizzie to Auntie Cunnington's for dinner. Lizzie & Lilian Helping to give Service of Song. The Reapers Hymn. Preacher Mr Ridley. Preacher at home Mr Wilson. Had to light the lamps but must have some better arrangements.

Monday 24 September: Digging Potatoes and getting few peas. Dad, Mother & I went to Sleaford took 150 eggs 30/-. took Chapel lamp. Met Mrs Phillips & got new blinds and Curtains for Chapel. Mother bought new Hat. Came home 4.30 train. Took big Trap brought 6 cwt. cake from Sleaford Stn. Miss Hammond had Lizzie's byke to go to Sleaford.

Tuesday 25 September: Zepps came two o'clock dropped two bombs, one on roadside one in far 7 acre, one Mr Phillip's Grassfield one Gibson's, one Elkington's, one Tyler's one unexploded between Fixter's & Phillip's. One Scotchman's one unexploded down Wood Lane. Auntie Liza and Miss Hammonds came. Woke us up, a dreadful shock but no one Hurt wonderful escapes. Got up. went to bed 4.30 I stayed up. Hundreds of people came to look. Did not rest very well.[25]

Wednesday 26 September: Went down Fen to get ton of Carrotts up, Dad, Lizzie, & I, Jim fetched them home. Came on rain. Lizzie & I went to look at Shell Hole at Tyler's, dropped right in bottom of drain. Everybody in Fen very much upset Bombs near to everyone but by the Providence of God no one was hurt. How thankful we are.

---

[25] The target appears to have been the Anwick landing ground as the bombs fell close to it.

Thursday 27 September: Jim took 1 ton Carrotts to Cranwell. Five soldiers digging at Shell Hole. Quarterly Meeting & H.F. at Ruskington. Dad & Tom came Home dinner, I went afternoon stayed Tea. Mr Lobb & Annie came up. I stayed with Lizzie & G. Mother rest went to H.F. Mr Godfrey speaking for Dad.

Friday 28 September: Dad & I went digging potatoes against 1st 9 acre gate. Mother & Dad went to Ruskington, Lilian to Mrs Godfrey's to Tea. Jim went to meet Her.

Saturday 29 September: Lilian went to Toms Blackberrying. Dad and I went digging Corners in the Potatoes ready for ploughing out. Took Jim down to mow reeds, brought 7 marrows Home. Cut my big one. Lizzie & Lilian went to Sleaford to take Mrs Godfrey some blackberries.

Sunday 30 September: School morn. Dad & I went to Cranwell H.F. Drove round by Knipton, I was Organist Preacher at Home Mr Richardson. Service at 5.30 did not have lights. Lizzie stayed with G.Mother. We arrived Home 8.30. Crowds of people came to look at Shell Hole. Culivators at work Pogsons.

Monday 1 October: Tenting Cows and mending bags till 9 o'clock. Dad and I went to Market. Thrashing Machine came. Misses Cunnington & friend & her little Girl came up.

Tuesday 2 October: Thrashing Wheat & started Barley Stack. Hilda Thurlby untying. Harry Lewin, Mr Hall & Mr Start helping us 8/- a day. Dave Rushby's machine Coles brought it Mr Thurlby with it. I helped Dad with corn.

Wednesday 3 October: Thrashing Peas, Beans, Rakings & Finished Barley Stack. Set to other stack.

Thursday 4 October: Wet Day could not thrash. We all went down the Fen in the rain to get 1/2 ton Carrotts up. Came a lot of rain. Lizzie went to Wes. H.F. Lilian & Jim to meet Her.

Friday 5 October: Thrashing Barley finished 3 o'clock, Mr Wainer came in place of Mr Hall. Jim took Carrots to

Cranwell, then took pony to Kirkby Laythorpe for seed beans from Mr C. Priestly (Little Hale). Pony got out found her against the Tanyard. Machine went to Gibsons.

Saturday 6 October: Started drawing Thack, Order came for Wheat to be put on, had to get it right from the back against Waggon wheel, It was a drag, brought Manure back took it to Uncle Joe's. Put $15^1/_2$ qrs. Wheat on rail. Lilian went to help to decorate for H.F. at 2 o'clock, I could not go. Mr & Mrs Godfrey & Kenneth came to Tea. Went to look at Shell Hole. Landing Stage and Chapel. Dad sold little Pigs 11@ £1, Beast £14-5/-. Lewis went Camping to Skegness 1 o'clock.

Sunday 7 October: Wet morning did not go to School. H.F. preacher Harry. Good Day Chapel full both times 54 at night Colls. 13/9 aft 11/5. I stayed Home with Grandmother. Got new blinds & Curtains for the door.

Monday 8 October: Dad & Jim took 7 qrs. Wheat to Stn. Uncle Joe fetched 3 bags. Dad & I went to Market, then to Kirkby Laythorpe for 1 qr. seed beans. Rained all the way Home. Lizzie cycled into Sleaford to get Hat retrimmed.

Tuesday 9 October: Dad, Lizzie & I went down Fen & got ton Carrots up. Ruth came to stay a little while George poorly.

Wednesday 10 October: Wet & Stormy, Dad & I started Thatching Barley Stack. H.F. Lilian stayed with Grandmother, Jim did not go to Tea. I went to Second Sitting Tea at 4.30 meeting 6.15 Not many to Tea takings £1-3-6. Chairman Mr Wm. Ravell, Speakers J. Couling & the Minister Colls 15/31/2. Goods sold 7/11. Sale over £4 best we have had. Total proceeds £8-0-10$^1/_2$ very good for it rained both days. Little daughter came to Mary's.

Thursday 11 October: Dad & I Thatching Wheat stack. Pension man brought Grandmother's Book. Mr

Hodkinson came to value damage to fowls etc. by Bombs. Mother went to see Baby. Lewis took 1 ton Carrotts to Cranwell.

Friday 12 October: Getting potatoes up Moore's Shed Field Dad, Lizzie & I, Lewis ploughed some out then we went to Billinghay.

Saturday 13 October: Getting Potatoes up Lilian & four Boys 2/- a day helping us Jim ploughed out & led away to lane end. took 8 loads.

Sunday 14 October: Dad & Lizzie went to Dorrington H.F. Lillian went aft to help Ruskington Choir give S. of Song. all came Home for Tea Preacher Minister, Preacher at Home Mr Lawson. Lizzie stayed with Grandmother. Ruth went to School with us.

Monday 15 October: Dad & I went to Market sold 100 eggs 22/2 bought 2 blouse lengths & wool to knit gloves. Lizzie blouse and skirt to Harriets. Bloxholme estate sale.

Tuesday 16 October: Lizzie went bean sowing. Dad, Mrs Vinter & I went in Carrots put 12 cwt up to go to Cranwell. Started a heap.

Wednesday 17 October: Getting Potatoes up Mrs Vinter came, came on rain aft got wet through. Jim & Lilian drove me to Dorrington H.F. Chairman Richie, Speakers Mr Lobb & I.

Thursday 18 October: Loaded Pony with 12 cwt Carrotts, Dad started to go to Cranwell with them & water cart, Trap was breaking down. Had to fetch Lewis Home to go & take them. Then Jim & Lizzie from bean sowing, & we went down Fen. Mrs Vinter had gone into Carrotts by Herself fetched Her back. got few Potatoes up against 1st 9 acre gate. Went & got 8 rows of Potatoes up 4 little load.

Friday 19 October: Getting Potatoes up Mrs Vinter helping us, 9 rows up. Mr Hudson brought warning Zepps were out, Heard Pattinsons buzzer 7 o'clock, did not go to bed till 2.30. They were about all night, but did not come here.

Uncle Joe's came up

Saturday 20 October: Getting Potatoes up, Lilian, H. Johnson, E. Vinter, H. Clipsham helping us. Got 4 good load up Jim helping Uncle Joe's to thrash. Lizzie & Lilian went to Red Cross Concert.

Sunday 21st October: Jim & Naomi went with me to Metheringham Fen H.F. started 12 o'clock arrived Home 9 o'clock. Chapel full blinds down Lamps lit all day. Preacher at Home Dad. Mr Lamyman took Eve Service.

Monday 22 October: Took Waggon load Barley to Stn.. they had no sheets,[26] Lewis had to bring it home again. Jim helped Uncle to thrash. Dad & I went to market took 1 qr. Peas to Hubbards & P. 50 eggs 12/6

Tuesday 23 October: Sowed Oats Bottom end of Old Seeds. Lizzie, I & Mrs Vinter went Carroting Got 1 ton ready for Cranwell. Lilian went to see Mrs Godfrey. Grandmother's birthday.

Wednesday 24 October: Finished getting Potatoes up Harrowed 1st time over Mrs Vinter helped us. Came on rain. Got wet, brought Carrots up Home. Very rough night.

Thursday 25 October: Lewis took Carrots to Cranwell. Jim finished dragging 7 acre wheat. Dad went to Billinghay with Pig stuff I soiled Potato Grave Arrons & Mighty Atoms. Started filling Shell Hole in, dressed Wheat for drilling.

Friday 26 October: Drilled 6 acres Wheat in 12 acre. I harrowed it in with Darkie. Mother went to see Mary Lizzie to fetch Her Home, bought some material for blouse.

Saturday 27 October: Put Barley on rail $25^1/_2$ qrs. Lizzie & I went and covered half of King Ed. Potato Grave. I went to see Mrs. Tyler. She was little better got the turn the Dr. thinks. Brought some swedes Home Dad & I went to the Shell Hole. Lewis brought load of rubbish from Hill side.

---

[26] Grain in an open waggon would have to be protected from the rain.

Finished one glove..

Sunday 28 October: School morn. I stayed home (aft). Preacher Minister Services 2 & 5.30 Mother stayed with Grandmother.

Monday 29 October: Burning thorns in 7 acre. Dad & I went to Market. Lilian cycled in dinner Hour for New Coat. Lizzie aft for trimming for Blouse Mr Godfrey came gave Lilian lesson in drawing.

Tuesday 30th October: I cycled down to Mrs Lockeys with Her clothes basket. Dad & I got 1 ton Carrots up. Lizzie began sowing. Lizzie and I went up to Harrietts.

Wednesday 31 October: Dad, Jim , I & Mrs Vinter started getting mangolds up. Band of Hope Meeting Joey leader Lizzie helper 37 present took 3 pledges.

Thursday 1 November: Jim took carrots to Cranwell. Lewis & Lizzie in beans. Dad, Mrs Vinter & I went & Harrowed Potato field took tops to Mangold grave. Mrs Robert Pattinson killed at Station by train went after her dog & did not notice train from Lincoln. Had just been in Marys Half an Hour.

Friday 2 November: Damp morning. Sowing beans. I bedded things, mended Byke, cut chaff etc. Insurance man came to look at damage done by Zepps. Dad went to Ruskington. Inquest on Mrs Pattinson. Aunt Eliza came up.

Saturday 3 November: Mr Fox came to kill little Pig. Finished sowing beans, Lewis & I drew furrows in 7 acre. Dad & Jim in Old Seeds & 12 acre I fetched some swedes. Harry & Children came up.

Sunday 4 November: School morn. Jim at Kirkby Green aft cycled with me to Rowston, Helped me in Eve Service. Mrs Pattinson buried, hundreds of people there, load of wreaths. Preacher at Home Mr Evans. Lizzie stayed with Grandmother.

Monday 5 November: Dad went down Fen Hedge Cutting I went pulling Mangolds, Came home to go to Market Lilian went with us to go to Mrs Godfreys with Her lessons I went with Her to School Mrs Godfrey showed us round. Mrs Key came to see Grandmother. Auntie Cunnington came, Lizzie washed & Ironed. Getting pig out of way .

Tuesday 6 November: Getting mangolds up Mrs Cook, Henry, Aggie Johnson & Ernest Vinter helping us, I pulled till 2 o'clock then Jim & I went in Carrots. Got 7 cwt up. Mother went to Mary's to Tea. Lizzie, Lilian & Jim to Chapel & Mary's to Supper. Baby Christened (Ida Margaret.)

Wednesday 7 November: Getting mangolds up Mrs Cook & Vinter helping us. Got 34 load up. Mrs Vinter & I got 15 cwt carrots up from 12.30 to 3 o'clock, Brought them up Home.

Thursday 8 November: Lewis took Carrots to Cranwell. Getting Mangolds up with two Carts. Mrs Cook & Vinter helping us. Came on stormy. Dad & Jim went to fence beast out at Ruskington.

Friday 9 November: Mangold carting. Mrs Cook & Vinter helping us. I pulled & Topped all day.

Saturday 10 November: Sent truck of Mangolds to Mr Stevenson 5 ton $6^1/_2$ with 1 cwt Carrots. Finished getting Mangolds up getting Carrots up in among. Boy helping us. Mr Godfrey came to give Lilian a drawing lesson.

Sunday 11 November: School morn, Then to Dorrington Walked. Aunt Eliza took me Brickyard way. Luie & Tommie came with me. Tom at Ruskington Preacher at Home Charlie Cutler.

Monday 12 November: Dad & I went down Fen burning thorns in Baldock's field. Came Home to go to Market took 80 eggs £1-2-9 bought Sunday Boots 23/6. Went to Vicars for Permit to sell Potatoes. Lizzie washed.

Tuesday 13 November: Lizzie & Mrs Cook & Mrs Vinter getting Carrots up. Dad cutting hedge & burning thorns in Baldocks field. Boys finished ploughing it. Jim fetched water.

Wednesday 14 November: Mrs Cook, Vinter, Lizzie & I carroting. Dad went to Billinghay for some Oats then came down Fen.

Thursday 15 November: Put Truck Mangolds on Bennetts. 4 ton 10 cwt. Drilled Baldock's field with wheat, I harrowed it with Darkie. Mrs Cook Vinter & Lizzie Carroting. Dad & I went aft. Preaching Service 6.30 very nice Service 26 present. Lewis did not go. Dad stayed with Grandmother. Sold two Beast £26.

Friday 16 November: Mrs Cook & Lizzie went potato picking after plough. Dad hedge cutting there till dinner then came to Mrs Vinter & I carroting. Lilian came Home from school poorly went back aft. I finished knitting my gloves.

Saturday 17 November: Lewis & Ernest Vinter put Truck Mangolds on for Stevensons 5 ton 11cwts. Hector Clipsham went picking potatoes after the plough. Dad, Lizzie & I Carroting. Dad followed drill for Mr Cook 5 rounds.

Sunday 18 November: School morn, Preacher Mr J. Couling. Dad went (aft) Jim stayed Home. Lilian stayed with Grandmother.

Monday 19 November: Lizzie I went Potato picking after plough Dad went down to burn thorns then Home to go to Market. Auntie & Uncle Joe's came up. Camp fires lit. (False alarm)

Tuesday 20 November: Started to drill little field with Oats, would not run had to sow them, picked up some potatoes. Lizzie, Mrs Vinter, Mrs Start carroting. Dad & I went aft got heap up.

Wednesday 21 November: Wet night. Went Carroting Mrs Start & Vinter helping me. I had my new Government Land Boots on. Cost me 12/-. Government allows 5/-.

Thursday 22 November: Went Carroting left them to go & pick potatoes up. Put truck Mangolds up 5 ton 16 cwt for Stevensons. Total 3 trucks 16 tons $13^{1}/_{2}$ cwt. @ 24/- per ton £19-19/-

Friday 23 November: Getting Carrots up. Drilled 2 acre Mangold land with Wheat.

Saturday 24 November: Put 25 cwt Potatoes up for Mr Wortley Bradford & 1 bag Carrots £9-8/-. Getting Carrots up aft, Ernest Vinter & Hector Clipsham helping us. Very rough had to walk Home.

Sunday 25 November: School morn. Rough & Stormy. Jim drove me to Heckington. Pony kicked so much Jim had to stay with Her. Light went out at Ewerby arrived Home 8 o'clock.

Monday 26 November: Very Sharp frost & bitterly cold. Lilian came rolling down stairs bruised Her hands & arms & head. Dad & I went to Market sold 77 eggs 3 for 1/- = 25/4[27] took 6 cockerels sold them 30/-. Lizzie washed. Came on rain & snowy.

Tuesday 27 November: I went down Fen cleaning swedes morn.

Wednesday 28 November: Finished Drilling Mangold land with wheat. Got ton Carrots up, Mrs Vinter, Lizzie Dad & I carrotting aft. B. of Hope, 29 present Naomi conducting Mr Lamyman Chairman.

Thursday 29 November: Dad had to meet Agricultural Comtte. Jim took 1 ton Carrots to Cranwell. Mrs Vinter, Start, Lizzie & I carrotting

Friday 30 November: Jim, Dad, Lizzie, Mrs Vinter, Mrs Start & I carroting got 2 heaps & a bit up, left half heap to finish.

Saturday 1 December: Dad & I went and finished Carrots then into swedes. Ernest Vinter & Hector Clipsham cleaning swedes. Lilian went to Mr Godfrey.

Sunday 2 December: School morn. Lizzie stayed with Mary all day she was poorly. Jim & Lilian fetched Her Home. I stayed with Grandmother. Preacher Mr Sleight Nocton.

Monday 3 December: Very Sharp frost. Dad & I went to Market took 75 eggs 25/- took Parrafin Cask to Bratleys got 1 gall. Mother Lizzie & I went to hear Mr Amos

---

[27] Perhaps one got broken!

42.

Cooling Lecture on Then who took the wrong turn. Richie Chairman. Mary much better.

Tuesday 4 December: Very Sharp frost. Dad, Jim & I went hedgeing & Dyking Bottom of 12 acre. Jack came to see us. Home on 10 days leave after being wounded in France.

Wednesday 5 December: Went to Dyke morn. Fed things aft. Jack went back to Flo's.

Thursday 6 December: I went to Dyke. Dad fetched Beast Home from Ruskington. Preaching Service. Very nice Service Dad stayed Home.

Friday 7 December: Dad & I went to Lincoln. Bought my Coat. Lizzie Muff & Fur (Bainbridges) stayed Mary's to Tea.

Saturday 8 December: I went down cleaning swedes. Mr Silson came & fastened Chaff Box. Mary, Harry & Children came.

Sunday 9 December: School morn. I went to Dorrington Wes. for Harry. Preacher at Home Mr Hewerdine. Dad stayed with Grandmother. Mr Burrows had stroke in Ruskington Pulpit just finishing His sermon, fell down steps to the right took Him Home. Did not regain consciousness.

Monday 10 December: Fed things. Dad & I went to Market took 50 eggs 7 for 2/-.Brought new Copper with grate & Parrafin. Lizzie washed.

Tuesday 11 December: Sharp frost. Mr Silson came mixing mortar etc. Dad & I put ton Carrots up for Cranwell. 1 cwt Carrots 5 cwt Potatoes for Mr Murray.

Wednesday 12 December: Sharp frost. Jim took Potatoes & Carrots to Stn. to send Home brought bricks, Potato bags etc. Mr Silson put new copper in. Dad, Jim & I went & soiled Carrot heaps. Cut chaff.

Thursday 13 December: Jim took Carrots to Cranwell. Dad, Lizzie & I went down fen putting Potatoes up. Lilian went to Dorrington to tell Tom's I could not go with them to Bobs. Would not go without me.

Friday 14 December: Dad & I went to finish Potatoes put Truck on 3 ton 2 cwt. Dad went to follow drill for Mr Cook. Jim went Home for His Holiday Dad[28] Home on leave.

Saturday 15 December: I went down Fen Cleaning swedes. Dad fetched them Home. Cultivators came to fish-pond field. Fed things aft.

Sunday 16 December: Snowy morn. I was planned Ruskington. Lilian & Dad started school, came back. Lilian came on to Ruskington. Lizzie went with me night, came a Blizzard when we came Home. Dad met us at Starts. Preachers at Home aft Mr Cook Eve Mr Lamyman.

Monday 17 December: Very sharp frost slippery. Cultivating. Killed Pig. Had to have Mr Stubley, Mr Fox couldn't come. Dad & I went to market took 60 eggs 17/-. Aunt Liza came Home with us.

Tuesday 18 December: Finished cultivating. Man came to cut Pig up. I boiled Fat up. Grind meat & helped generally. Made sausages.

Wednesday 19 December: Fed things. Very Frosty. Lewis went & fetched load of Carrots for things, could not get swedes. Cut chaff for stock & Horses. Washed & Churned.

Thursday 20 December: I went to see Mr Phillips to see if He could truck mangolds on too Frosty. Fed things went to see if Aunt Eliza would tell Tom's[29] I could go to Bob's tomorrow.

Friday 21 December: Tom's had been to Welbourn so I did not go. Fed things mixed mangolds for 2 days. Mother, Lizzie & I went to School party. It was very nice indeed. Lilian broke up for a fortnight from school.

Saturday 22 December: I went down Fen to clean swedes could not get them up the ground too hard. Came home, went

---

[28] Jim's Dad implied.
[29] Tom's family implied.

to fetch Darkie with some mangolds, to let Lewis stop Hedge cutting. Fed things mixed mangolds (aft) Mr Murray sent me two books. Frosty all week.

Sunday 23 December: School morn. Mrs Flintham sent a Card each for Children. Preacher Tom. Lilian stayed Home.

Monday 24 December: Dad, Lilian & I went to Market. Lilian went to Mrs Godfreys, left Her Bag, Had to go back. Stayed to meet Jim 4.30 train Had been poorly half His holiday not well yet. Ruth Hung up Her stocking Santa filled it up & put a Dolly in a parcel. Lilian got wristlet watch. Locket for Her chain. Lizzie pr. Slippers, fancy plate. Dad bought us each a pocket Handkerchief. Auntie came up to fetch Henry's Santa. Hung my stocking up & went to bed.

Tuesday 25 December: Ruth got up with Lilian & I sent Her with candle to look at Stocking look at it & sent her back to bed. Santa brought me some photo Frames, a 3d piece etc. Lewis & Jim handkerchiefs Etc. Grandmother biscuits, sweets soap Card. Mother photo Frame Comb etc. Dad Pipe Tobacco & matches. Mrs Murray sent me Book (Come Ye apart) Lizzie 3 handkerchiefs Dad 4. Mother Lavender Bag. Went to Service Ruskington Preacher Minister Arthur Organist Lovely Service. Uncle Joe's came for dinner went Home 12 pm

Wednesday 26 December: I Had bad cold. Lilian got up & milked, I didn't go out at all. Parcel came from Leeds. 10/- from Cousin Jack for Grandmother. L.M. here Present Bros. Richie, Tom, Dixon, W. Kelley. Thurlby, Copping, Minster, Annie & Emmie Cutler. Luie & Little Tommy came. Emmie & W. Kelly passed their Exam. Mr Copping & Richie went Home others stayed Tea. Mr Lobb & Annie overnight. played Quoits till nearly midnight went to bed between 1 & 2 o'clock a.m. Lewis went to volunteer Tea.

Thursday 27 December: Lilian went to Mr W. Philips for 1 lb
butter Auntie for $^1/_2$ lb. Took 4lb to post for Mr Wortley.
A bonnet for Dorothy. Harry, Dad Boys & Mr Silson
working at Canada Kidding and hauling trees.[30] Mr Lobb.
Annie & I went to look stayed till dinner. Marys came up
for day was going to stay overnight. Letter to say Sam &
Ada & Baby were coming so Had to go Home. Mr Lobb &
Annie went home aft. Auntie & Annie came then Tom.
Lizzie went to Stn. to meet 4.30 train. They came but
went to Tongs to Tea.

Friday 28 December: Sam & Ada did not come till this morn.
Went to Canada getting trees out. B. of H. Meeting
Chairman Syd Thompson. Very good meeting 31 present.
Syd. stayed till 11 o'clock.

Saturday 29 December: Not very well. Influenza did not get up
till tea time. Lilian went to have Tea with Blanche. My
head aches dreadfully.

Sunday 30 December: Did not go out all day. Preacher
Minister Went to Mr Phillips to Tea. Mrs Flintham sent
all the scholars a mince pie.

Monday 31 December: Did not go out. Had a very bad night.
Lizzie went with Dad to Market. Lilian Storeman. Auntie
& Annie came to Tea.

---

[30] Canada seems to have been the name of a field or area in the Fen. A kid is
an old name for a faggot or bundle of sticks, we can assume therefore that
kidding means collecting firewood. Mr George Phillips remembers his father
using kids to enliven the fire in the forge of the wheelwrights shop. Even
today deep ploughing reveals the blackened trunks of ancient trees which
once grew in the Fen. 'Hauling trees' probably refers to these Bog Oaks
rather than living trees, see also December 28th which says 'getting trees
out' i.e. digging rather than sawing down.

Tuesday 1 January 1918: Helping in the House. Wash Day. Mr Silson came & did the Pantry Ceiling. Miss Ellen Phillips married at Grantham. Lilian went to Mary's to Tea.

Wednesday 2 January: Went to feed things. Lilian helped me to mix some stuff. Marys came stayed overnight.

Thursday 3 January: Mary & children went Home came a little snow. Mixed some stuff for things. Lewis came back.

Friday 4 January: Lizzie very poorly with Billiousness. I ironed morn. Lilian helped me mix some stuff aft. Mother went to Mrs Cunningtons for Tea. Lilian & Jim fetched Her Home.

Saturday 5 January: I went down Fen cleaning Swedes. Dad & Jim to Canada. Lizzie much better. Lizzie went out for weekend. Mr Pell buried.

Sunday 6 January: School morn. Preacher aft Mr Clay. Night Dad. Intercessory & Memorial Service National Day of Prayer.

The close of the year 1917 finds us still in the grip of the worlds struggle for freedom, nor, as far as we can see, are we nearer the end than at the close of 1916, indeed in some respects we are worse off than then. The submarine warfare makes it very difficult to get the food over & many things are scarce & difficult to obtain, as Butter, Margarine, Lard, Parrafin, Sugar etc etc. It is almost impossible to get butter in the towns & we are constantly having requests from friends to let them have some butter, but what little we have we are beseiged for here. We being farmers are among the most fortunate as we grow many necessary articles of food, but in the towns people stand for hours waiting for admission into shops, & then often cannot get even necessary food. One great blessing is, mostly people are at working & earning good wages, but even money cannot buy the things that are not. Many things are very much dearer & the prices still increase. We now have Sugar Cards entitling us to 1/2 lb sugar each. Lard we have 1/2 lb a week for 9 of us. Parrifin we get a little when we can & have managed very well till now. All Wheat & Barley have to go for bread and only worst hinderends[31] could be used for feeding pigs & consequently they have to be killed before they are anything like fat. So far we have been able to get as much beef as we have wanted, but now the butcher who usually kills three beast a week is allowed half of one, so we expect to go short & are expected to have one meatless day a week. The Agricultural War Committee come round at intervals & order grassland to be broken up and sown with corn & dykes to be done out etc. The Fish Pond field is ordered to be broken up & Uncle cannot do it, so Dad has taken it off His hands & had it cultivated. The Potatoes we could not sell without a license from government & only at their price £6 per ton, then as they

---

[31]*Hinderends are the small and broken grains which are separated from the good grains by the threshing machine.

are plentiful you may sell them cheaper & then apply to government for what you are short of the £6. Farmers do not like that way. Petrol can only be got by special Licence. Carbyde[32] cannot be bought at all. All newspapers & Magazines have increased 1/2d more.

Cost of Various Articles at the close of the year 1917

Bread 9d Loaf of 4 lbs Made of Wheat Barley Oats Beans Maize flour & Potatoes
Butter 2/5 per lb
Margarine 1/4 per lb (Government controlled)
Milk 5d per qt
Eggs 7 for 2/-
Lard 1/6 a lb (Government controlled)
Currants 1/10 per lb
Tea 3/8 per lb
Bacon (Government Fixed Price)
Beef from 1/- to 2/2 per lb (Government Fixed Price)
Matches 1d a box Given out in boxes not packets
Candles 2/5 a packet
Sugar 61/2d a lb; Such as you can get White or Brown (Fixed)
Lump a luxury
Soap 1/3 a box (Sunlight)
Parrafin 1/11 to 2/4 gall
Coal 31/- per ton (Fixed Price)
Newspaper (Daily) 1d
Magazine 11/2d
Raisins unobtainable

Boots, anything from 15/- to 30/- Not very good at that.
Wool 7d an oz Gloves & Stockings (very mean)
Wheat 73/- per qr
Barley from 62/- to 65/-
The End.

---

[32] 'Carbyde' this refers to Calcium Carbide which was used to provide the gas acetylene which was burnt in cycle lamps.

It is sad to record that Jane Glenn died of influenza in the great epidemic which followed the war, her grave is marked by a stone cross in Ruskington cemetery and bears the following inscription.

JANE

BELOVED DAUGHTER OF

H.R. & M.A. GLENN

FELL ASLEEP IN JESUS DEC 12 1918

AGED 34 YEARS